Learning to BE POSITIVE! will improve your:

SELF-ESTEEM

SELF-CONFIDENCE

BODY IMAGE

WORLDVIEW

Your brain works astronomically hard to keep up with your growing body, sometimes making you feel clumsy or uncomfortable and affecting the way you see yourself and the world around you.

Don't worry, it's normal to lose a bit of confidence and feel unsure about yourself for a while.

UNDER CONSTRUCTION!

As you deliberately notice the good things all around you, you'll rewire your brain to BE POSITIVE! more often. This book was written to give you loads of ideas about how to do this and how to feel better.

Imagine how great you're going to feel now that you can BE POSITIVE!

YOU'VE GOT THE POWER!

Fill in and color the countdown to get started!

10 9 8

YOU'VE GOT THE POWER

How positive do you feel right now?

Here are some words or phrases that are used throughout the book.

Read the definition and then color each battery to show if you're feeling negative, positive, or somewhere in between. Start at the negative end and color until you reach your personal power point.

SELF-ESTEEM

How you view yourself as a person, and what you feel, think, and believe about yourself and about how others think of you. What you believe about your value to others and the world around you, and what you deserve from them.

NEGATIVE
I'm awful, I get everything wrong.

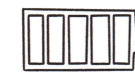

POSITIVE
I make mistakes, but I learn from them and keep trying.

SELF-CONFIDENCE

How you act in the world because of what you see, feel, think, and believe about yourself.

NEGATIVE
I don't like to try new things.

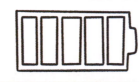

POSITIVE
I love a new challenge.

BE POSITIVE!

AN ACTIVITY BOOK FOR YOUNG PEOPLE WHO WANT TO FEEL MORE SELF-CONFIDENT

Kane Miller
A DIVISION OF EDC PUBLISHING

First American Edition 2020
Kane Miller, A Division of EDC Publishing

© 2020 Studio Press
Written by Dr. Sharie Coombes, Child, Family & Adult Psychotherapist,
Ed.D, MA (PsychPsych), DHypPsych(UK), Senior QHP, B.Ed.
Illustrated by Ellie O'Shea
Designed by Rob Ward
Edited by Frankie Jones

First published in the UK in 2020 by Studio Press,
an imprint of Bonnier Books UK

For information contact:
Kane Miller, A Division of EDC Publishing
PO Box 470663
Tulsa, OK 74147-0663
www.kanemiller.com
www.edcpub.com
www.usbornebooksandmore.com

Library of Congress Control Number: 2019952410

Printed in China
3 5 7 9 10 8 6 4 2

ISBN: 978-1-68464-123-9

BE POSITIVE!

THIS BOOK BELONGS TO

_ _ _ _ _ _ _ _ _ _ _

WELCOME TO BE POSITIVE!

Author
DR. SHARIE COOMBES
Child and Family Psychotherapist

We all feel like we don't measure up from time to time and this fun activity book is a great way to get you thinking and talking about the things that bother you, so you can get on with being the real, amazing you and get back to enjoying life.

Doing these activities will help you to feel more positive and self-assured, understand and combat your negative feelings, learn about and improve your self-esteem and confidence, and talk to others about your worries (if you want to). You could use this book in a quiet, comfortable place where you can think and feel relaxed, and it's up to you which pages you do. You might do a page a day if that's what you want to do, or complete lots of pages at once. You can start anywhere in the book and even come back to a page many times. There are no rules!

Sometimes we can feel so stuck that we start to believe nothing will help, but there is always a solution to every problem. Nothing is so big that it can't be sorted out or talked about, even if it feels that way. You could show some of these activities to important people in your life to help explain how you are feeling and to get help with what is upsetting you. You can always talk to an adult you trust at school or ask an adult at home to take you to the doctor to help sort out any problems.

Lots of children need a bit of extra help every now and then, and here are three organizations you can turn to if you don't want to talk to people you know. They have helped thousands of children with every kind of problem and will know how to help you. They won't be shocked by what you tell them, however bad it feels to you.

CHILDHELP

Childhelp is dedicated to looking after children. Their free, confidential help line puts you in touch with a counselor any time, day or night.

Tel: 1-800-422-4453

www.childhelp.org

CRISIS TEXT LINE

Crisis Text Line serves anyone, in any time of crisis, by providing access to free, 24/7 support and information via text message from a trained crisis counselor.

Text HOME to 741741
(Text lines are open 24/7. There is no charge if your cell phone plan is with AT&T, T-Mobile, Sprint, or Verizon. For other carriers, standard text message rates apply.)

www.crisistextline.org

YOUR LIFE YOUR VOICE

Offers universal crisis portals for children/ youth by phone, text, and online, to reach qualified professional crisis counselors.

Tel: 1-800-448-3000 (24 hours)
www.yourlifeyourvoice.org
Text VOICE to 20121 to start a text conversation, open every day, 11 AM to 1 AM CST.

BIGGER, BRAVER, STRONGER, SMARTER

Growing up is exciting!

Every day, you learn or discover something new about yourself and the world, and you can try new things you couldn't do before.

Sometimes, growing up also feels challenging. Family, friends, and teachers ask more from you. You get bigger, braver, stronger, and smarter – and so do your friends.
You all do this in your own way and in your own time.

Your friends will have different strengths and talents than you.

It's a fact of life that no one's perfect or talented at everything, and no one is positive all the time. Sometimes you'll have sad, angry, frustrated, worried, or other negative feelings. When these show up, it's good to recognize them, notice why they've surfaced, and be kind to yourself. But it's important to make sure they don't stick around for too long.

Your brilliant body experiences a huge range of feelings every day from the emotions that blast off in nanoseconds in your brain because of what it sees, feels, thinks, and believes.

LOOK OUT FOR THE THINKING POINTS THROUGHOUT THE BOOK. THESE ARE IDEAS FOR YOU TO THINK ABOUT FURTHER, OR DISCUSS WITH A FRIEND OR ADULT.

BODY IMAGE

How you see your body and appearance and what you feel, think, and believe about these, and about how others see them.

NEGATIVE
I always
look dreadful.

POSITIVE
This sweater
really suits me.

WORLDVIEW

How you expect things to work out in your life and in the world around you.

NEGATIVE
I bet I lose
the game.

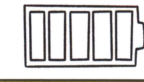

POSITIVE
If I play my best,
I might win.

You can build up your BE POSITIVE! power.

Come back and update this page every time you feel a shift upward!

Doing more of the activities in this book will boost it even further.

Remember or imagine having to do something difficult when your confidence is high and you feel proud and positive. What is it?

_____

_____

Draw on this picture to show how it makes you feel and where you feel it. You can use the suggested feelings or make up your own.

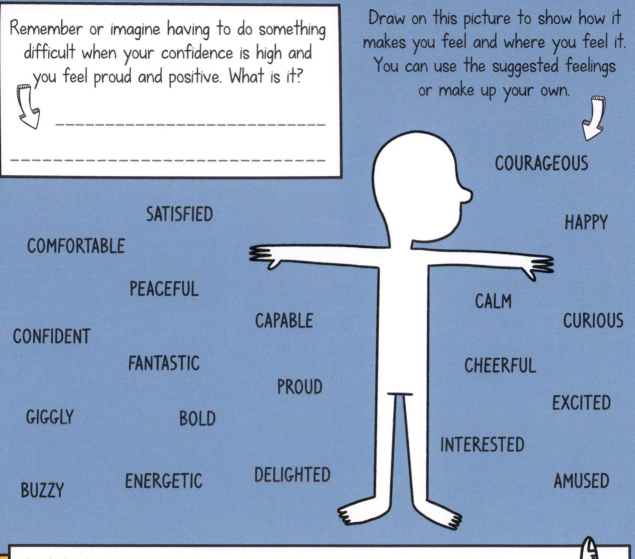

COURAGEOUS

HAPPY

SATISFIED

COMFORTABLE

PEACEFUL

CALM

CAPABLE

CURIOUS

CONFIDENT

FANTASTIC

CHEERFUL

PROUD

EXCITED

GIGGLY

BOLD

INTERESTED

BUZZY

ENERGETIC

DELIGHTED

AMUSED

Look back at your negative picture and remember or imagine that time again. Keep thinking about that time, then look at this positive picture until you feel confident about that old situation.

WELL DONE - you've just rewired your brain to BE POSITIVE! You've got this, and next time, it will be easier to BE POSITIVE!

THINKING POINT:

What is the difference when you are confident? How does it change your experience? Try explaining this to a friend or adult, or write about it if you want to.

EYE MATTER

Our eyes are windows to who we are and how we're feeling. Everyone's eyes are different – get to know yours by looking at them closely in a mirror.

Notice the colors, shapes, patterns, lashes, sparkle, and shine of your eyes.

Draw and color them here:

Making eye contact with others helps us to be and feel understood.

Ask someone else to sit still in front of you so that you can get to know their eyes, and then draw them with the same attention to detail.

If you prefer, you could use a photograph of a person or animal instead.

See if you can work out how they are feeling by the look in their eyes.

SNAZZY SHADES

Color these snazzy shades however you like and use them to protect your eyes from negativity for a confidence boost.

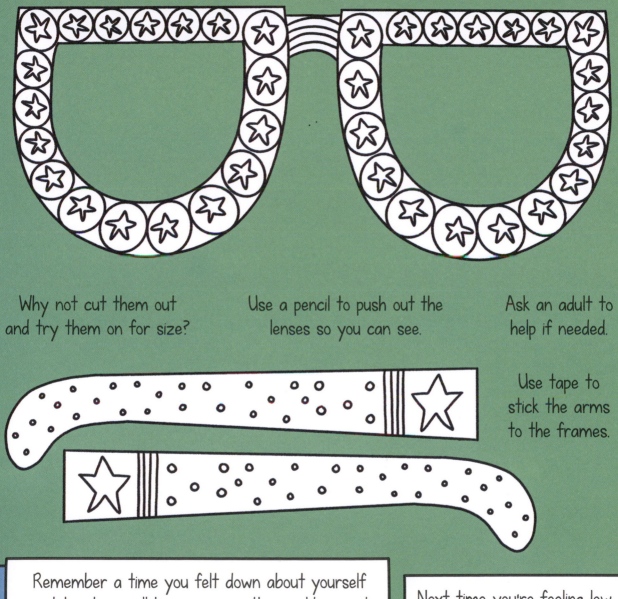

Why not cut them out and try them on for size?

Use a pencil to push out the lenses so you can see.

Ask an adult to help if needed.

Use tape to stick the arms to the frames.

Remember a time you felt down about yourself and try to recall how you saw the world around you then. Now go back to that time and imagine putting on your shades to see how they change the way you feel about yourself and how you act.

Next time you're feeling low, imagine putting on these shades, as you feel and act more confident.

GET CHANGED

What big or little changes have happened to you recently?

Make a list here and color the ▭ if it was a negative change or the ✚ if it was a positive change. Some changes might be both.

HOME

SCHOOL

LOST SOMETHING OR SOMEONE

PET

CLASS

GROWN OUT OF YOUR FAVORITE SHOES

CLUB

FRIEND

POSITIVE

NEGATIVE

Pick one of your positive changes and say how it has made things better for you.

Now pick one of your negative changes – let's work out how you can flip it and make it feel more positive. What help do you need? Who can help you?

YOU'RE INCREDIBLE!

Ask your friends and family what they find special about you and write their thoughts here.

Add your own ideas to the list too.

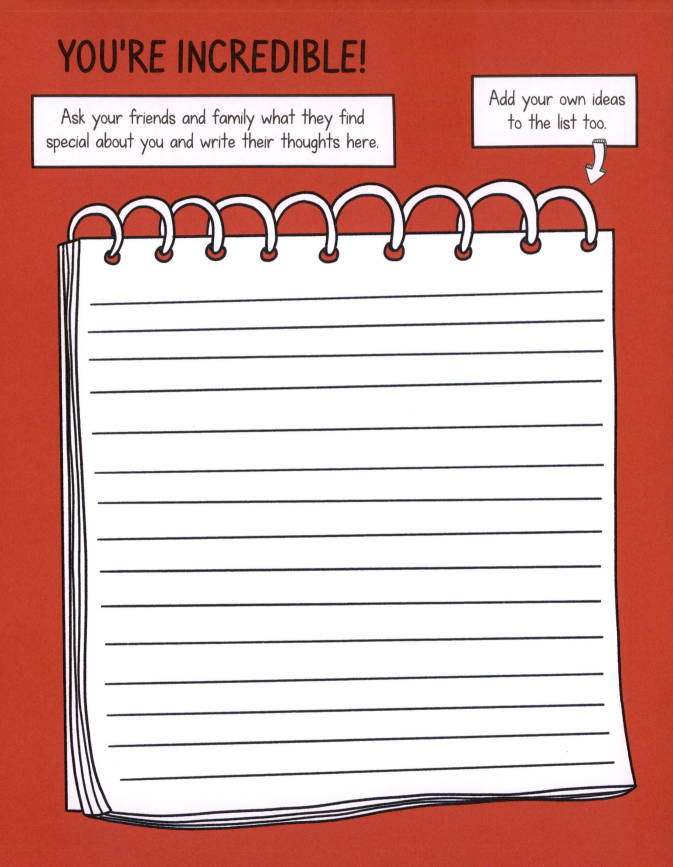

Fill in these rosettes with the special strengths and qualities you're most proud of from the list.

Write the name of the person who said it on the ribbon.

KIND AND CARING

A GOOD LISTENER

TELLS FUNNY JOKES

Award yourself all these in an imaginary ceremony. Make sure you notice how proud the audience members are and how loudly they are cheering for you.

WORLDVIEW

What's your worldview?

Color the world however you like.

THINKING POINT:

Did you know that your worldview is influenced by:

- Your family's worldview
- Your cultural background
- Experiences you've had
- Your close relationships

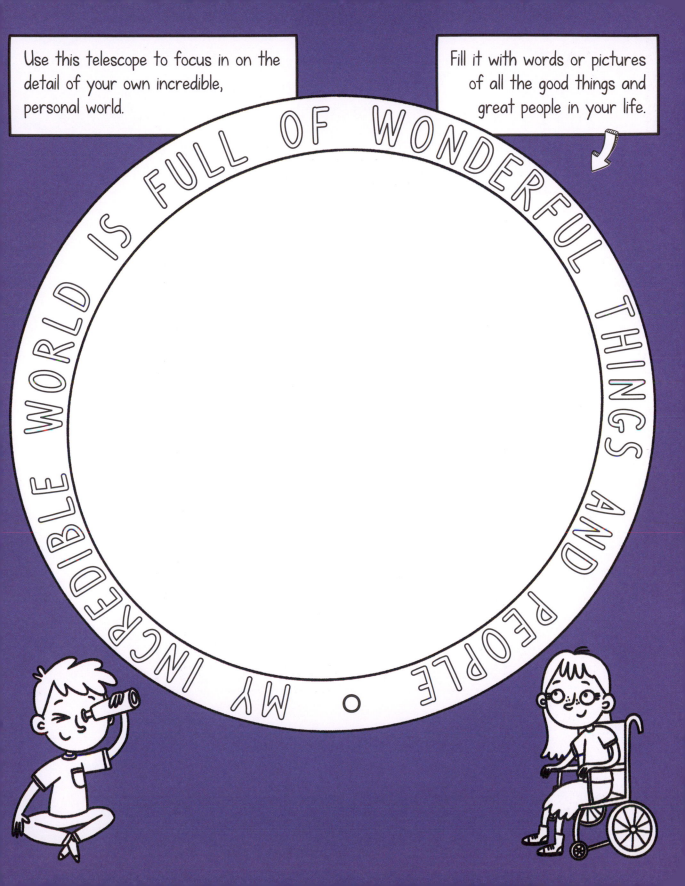

Use this telescope to focus in on the detail of your own incredible, personal world.

Fill it with words or pictures of all the good things and great people in your life.

MY INCREDIBLE WORLD IS FULL OF WONDERFUL THINGS AND PEOPLE

THIS IS ME!

Spend a bit of me time!

Draw yourself looking exactly how you want the world to see you.

Perhaps you're doing something you love, or striking a fun pose!

Notice how good you feel about yourself when you're seen for who you really are.

What would you like to hear other people say about you?

Write these things all over the page if you like.

KIND MIND

A kind mind can help you focus on what's positive in your life, see things differently, and improve your self-esteem and confidence.

TRY IT OUT!

Do you tell yourself negative things?

Do you blame yourself for things?

Is it hard to think you did well or deserve nice things?

If so, you need to learn how to speak more kindly to yourself.

I'm having a difficult day.   My friend is coming over later.

I'm terrible at_____   I'm great at _____

I don't like my _____   I like my _____

_____   _____

_____   _____

_____   _____

_____   _____

Next time you think something negative about yourself, call up your kind mind and turn things around.

Your kind mind has already rewired your brain to notice the positive things in the future – keep practicing!

LUCKY STARS

Fill in these lucky stars with the things and people you feel thankful to have in your life.

FRIENDS

COMFY BED

Unkindness may happen and things will sometimes go wrong, but with your positive power and people to support you, you can be confident and happy!

SPACE RACE

UP FOR A CHALLENGE?

Take each rocket on a space journey, using one long scribble without taking your pen or pencil off the page. You decide where the journey stops.

BONUS! When you've flown all your rockets, color in any cool patterns you've made.

REACH FOR THE STARS!

Whenever things aren't going well, or you need a confidence boost, reach for the stars.

Your body will enjoy the challenge, and you'll feel more positive in no time!

Play some music if you like, to give yourself a beat to move to.

STARBURSTS

Stretch your hands up high above your head and make two fists.

Open and close your fists 30 times, as fast as possible. Keep both hands in time with each other, or alternate them.

STAR TURNS

Stand with your feet slightly apart and your arms stretched up and out so you look like a star. Take your right hand and put it down on your left foot. Straighten up. Now take your left hand and put it down on your right foot. Straighten up.

Keep going like this for a whole minute!

STAR JUMPS

Now go back to standing with your feet slightly apart and your arms stretched out like a star. Jump up and, as you land, bring your feet together with your hands on your hips. Jump up again and go back into your star shape.

Repeat, and see if you can keep going for two minutes.

Put a check in a box each time you complete one of the activities.

STARBURSTS								
STAR TURNS								
STAR JUMPS								

ALIEN FRIENDS

This alien is a long way from home, and everything here looks strange.

Color it in and draw some friends for it to hang out with.

What is it about YOU that would make them want to be friends with you?

ROCKET MISSION

Mistakes make you learn faster
and go further, like a rocket.

Fill these rockets with mistakes you've
made that helped your brain get stronger.

Add extra rockets if you want to.

Forgot
something
important -
made me
more
organized

Lifting weights makes your muscles stronger. Your brain is like a muscle and gets stronger and smarter every time you make a mistake.

THINKING POINT:

How did these mistakes make your brain stronger and smarter? Write it in or talk it through with someone if you want.

BREATHE POSITIVE

If your positivity needs a quick boost, try these breathing exercises to help you feel more confident.

Let your body show you how amazing it is – and how amazing you are.

3:5 BREATHING

This works wherever you are and whatever you are doing. The best part is that no one will know you're doing it, so if you need to boost your inner positivity without being noticed, give it a try.

If you want to, you could close your eyes while you do it.

Get comfortable, in a sitting position.

Notice your body breathing in and out.

After a few breaths, start to count along with yourself, making your in breath last for the count of three and your out breath last for the count of five, breathing smoothly.

Keep going for as long you want to, or until you feel great.

POWERFUL HANDS

Pick a quiet, calm spot and lie down.

Close your eyes and picture yourself in a lovely, cozy place.

Breathe deeply and slowly.

Now, focus all your attention on your hands and imagine you are warming them up.

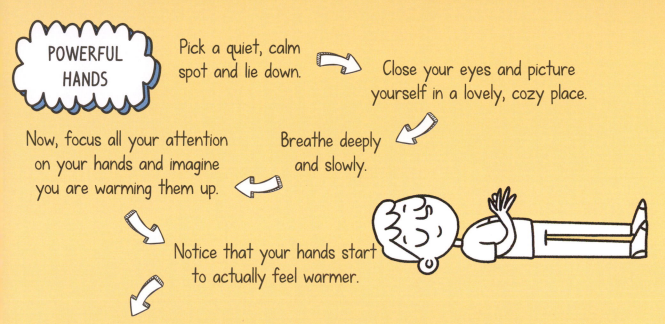

Notice that your hands start to actually feel warmer.

When you've mastered this skill, try spreading the warm feeling up your arms and down into your tummy. You'll be feeling positive and confident in no time!

FINGER BREATHING

This is a really "handy" skill! Spread one hand out on your knee or a table.

If you prefer, you can use the picture of the hand. Notice your body breathing in and out.

Take your pointer finger from your other hand, and put it on the bottom knuckle of your thumb. Slowly trace up to the tip, breathing in as you do, then stop at the top, hold your breath for a second, and trace back down the other side while you breathe out.

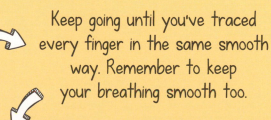

Keep going until you've traced every finger in the same smooth way. Remember to keep your breathing smooth too.

Repeat this six times, and make sure all your attention is on your hand and your breath.

ME, MYSELF & I

You are more than what you look like or what you can do.

Complete these sentences by writing things that you feel, think, or believe about yourself.

I'm afraid of

_____

I have a natural talent for

_____

I can't stand

_____

I'm loved by

_____

I feel good when

_____

I'm interested in

_____

I feel frustrated when

_____

I don't believe in

_____

I'm good at

_____

I worry about

_____

I'm proud of myself for

_____

If you want to, you could try to decide more things that you think, feel, and believe.

SCORES ON THE DOORS

These doors will open up your self-esteem.

Write your scores on the doors anywhere, from 0 to 7.

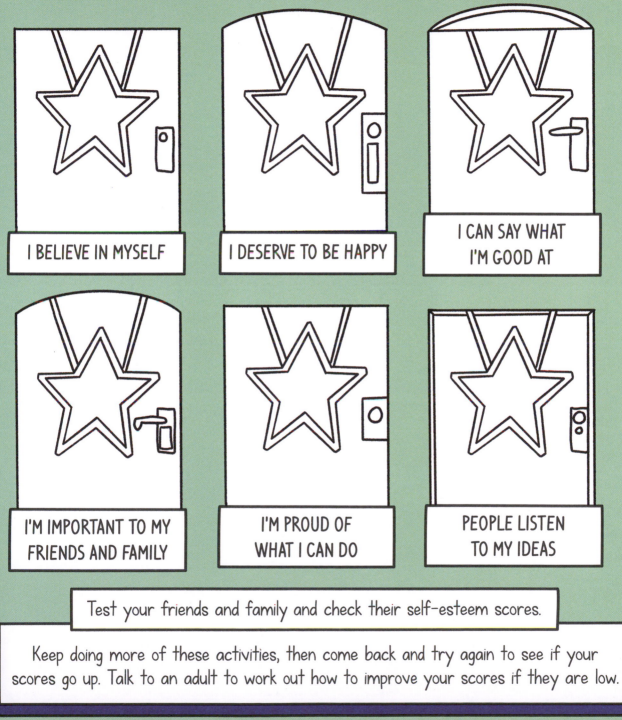

I BELIEVE IN MYSELF

I DESERVE TO BE HAPPY

I CAN SAY WHAT I'M GOOD AT

I'M IMPORTANT TO MY FRIENDS AND FAMILY

I'M PROUD OF WHAT I CAN DO

PEOPLE LISTEN TO MY IDEAS

Test your friends and family and check their self-esteem scores.

Keep doing more of these activities, then come back and try again to see if your scores go up. Talk to an adult to work out how to improve your scores if they are low.

WRONG IS ALRIGHT

Make deliberate mistakes all over this page and don't erase them.

If you accidentally make a mistake, that's even better!

$3+3=8$

BE POISTIVE

WRONG IS ALL WRITE

Be as creative as you can be!

You could show this page to friends and see if they can spot the mistakes – but don't change them!

STAR AS YOU ARE

Your brain is full of star-shaped cells, so you're already a star, just as you are.

Write or draw something about you or something you've done that you're proud of in this star, and add color and patterns if you want to.

JAZZY JAR OF JOY

Want to capture some joyful feelings?

Why not make a jar of joy?

You will need: a jar with a lid, some small strips of paper, pens, glue, stickers, magazine pictures, buttons, sequins, or anything fancy that you would like to decorate the jar with.

The world is full of beautiful things

Life can be great

I can and I will

Happy days ahead

I am loved

Write 31 joyful messages on the strips of paper – you could ask your friends and family to help. Fold them and put them in the jar.

Take out a joyful message whenever you need a smile and read it to yourself out loud three times.

Why not start every day by picking out a joyful message and inviting your family to join in? Making it a daily activity will rewire your brain to BE POSITIVE!

COLOR THIS IN!

LIST ALL THE PEOPLE, PETS, AND
THINGS YOU ARE IMPORTANT TO:

I AM

IMPORTANT

TRUE COLORS

Fill in the blanks on these pages to let the world know what makes you feel different things, what you do and who you really are. You could even show them to people you trust.

_____
makes me smile.

_____
makes me frustrated.

_____
makes me laugh.

_____
makes me cry.

_____
makes me delighted.

_____
makes me furious.

_____
makes me happy.

_____
makes me sad.

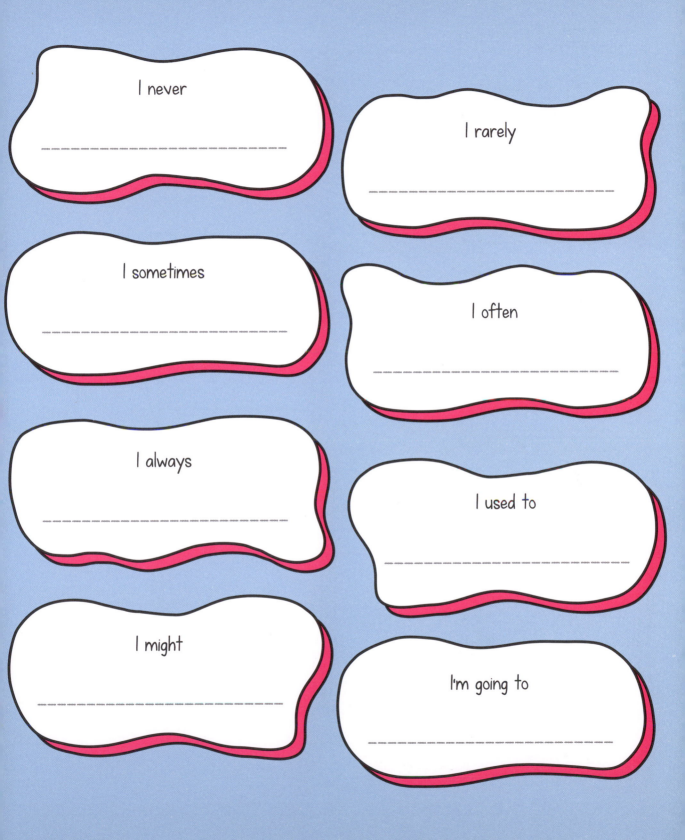

I never

_____

I rarely

_____

I sometimes

_____

I often

_____

I always

_____

I used to

_____

I might

_____

I'm going to

_____

NAMES IN THE FRAMES

When people make you feel great, you should spend as much time as you can with them.

Fill these frames with whoever makes you feel great!

Write their name under their picture and add a positive comment about each one.

Remember to include people from all parts of your life, like family, pets, school, clubs ...

Write a letter to someone who has helped you **BE POSITIVE!**

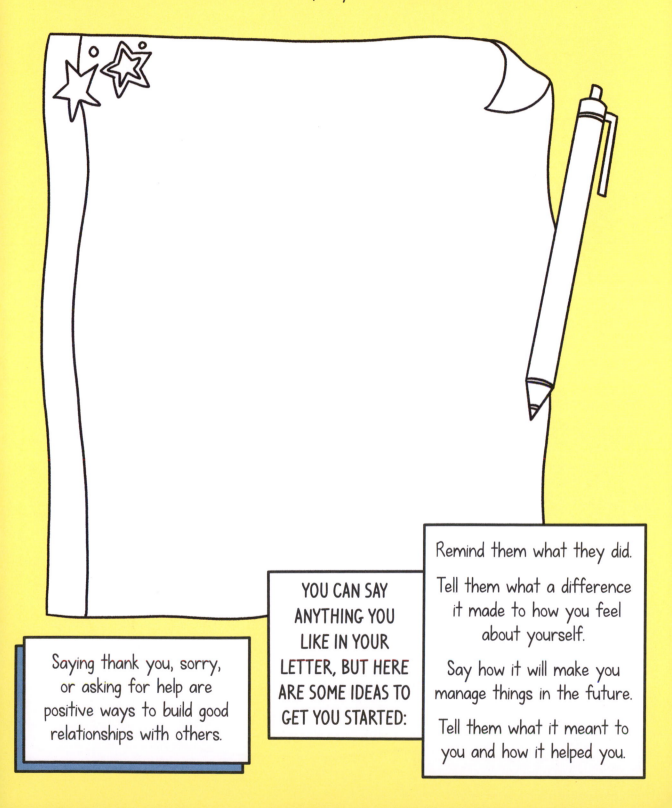

Saying thank you, sorry, or asking for help are positive ways to build good relationships with others.

YOU CAN SAY ANYTHING YOU LIKE IN YOUR LETTER, BUT HERE ARE SOME IDEAS TO GET YOU STARTED:

Remind them what they did.

Tell them what a difference it made to how you feel about yourself.

Say how it will make you manage things in the future.

Tell them what it meant to you and how it helped you.

BODY POSITIVE

Some words just sound SUPER positive and bring you joy.

Color this sweater while you enjoy the sight and sound of words, and how they make you feel.

Fill this picture with your choice of words that you love to read, write, or hear about yourself, and see how they help you BE POSITIVE!

Why not come back to this picture and say a couple of the words to yourself the next time you feel low or are being down on yourself?

TIME AFTER TIME

Write or draw a time when you were feeling confident and positive.

Really remember what you were thinking at the time as you do it.

This activity will rewire your brain to **BE POSITIVE!**

Who noticed you were positive?

How did it make you act?

What's stopping you from feeling and acting that way now?

What help do you need to get back to feeling positive?

Every time you feel your confidence slip or you find it hard to believe in yourself, come back to this page and get a boost!

IT'S ALL ABOUT YOU!

Fill this page with compliments that friends, family, or adults give you about your personality, actions, kindness, skills, appearance – or anything else.

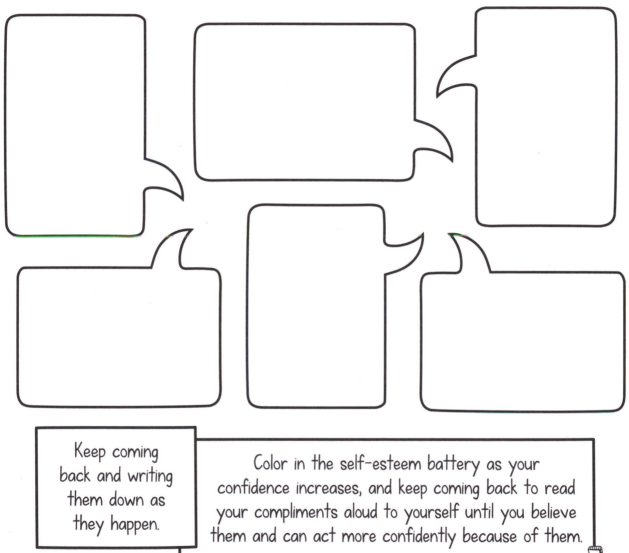

Keep coming back and writing them down as they happen.

Color in the self-esteem battery as your confidence increases, and keep coming back to read your compliments aloud to yourself until you believe them and can act more confidently because of them.

THINKING POINT:

Which compliments mean the most to you?

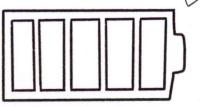

POSITIVE PEBBLES

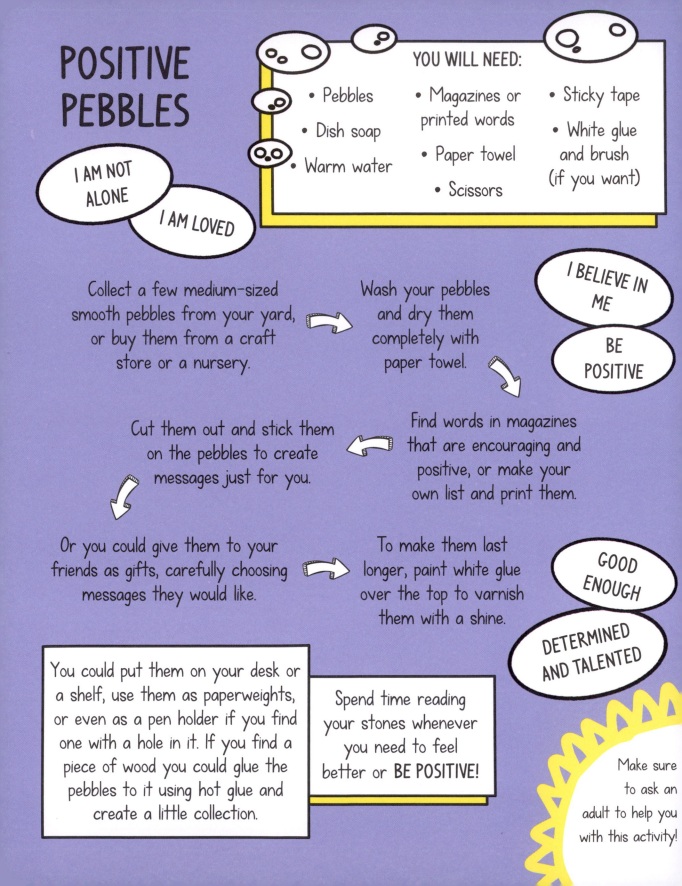

YOU WILL NEED:

- Pebbles
- Dish soap
- Warm water
- Magazines or printed words
- Paper towel
- Scissors
- Sticky tape
- White glue and brush (if you want)

I AM NOT ALONE

I AM LOVED

Collect a few medium-sized smooth pebbles from your yard, or buy them from a craft store or a nursery.

Wash your pebbles and dry them completely with paper towel.

I BELIEVE IN ME

BE POSITIVE

Cut them out and stick them on the pebbles to create messages just for you.

Find words in magazines that are encouraging and positive, or make your own list and print them.

Or you could give them to your friends as gifts, carefully choosing messages they would like.

To make them last longer, paint white glue over the top to varnish them with a shine.

GOOD ENOUGH

DETERMINED AND TALENTED

You could put them on your desk or a shelf, use them as paperweights, or even as a pen holder if you find one with a hole in it. If you find a piece of wood you could glue the pebbles to it using hot glue and create a little collection.

Spend time reading your stones whenever you need to feel better or **BE POSITIVE!**

Make sure to ask an adult to help you with this activity!

NATURE WATCH

Spending time in nature is really good for your brain and body. It can slow your heart rate, reduce stress, and develop your worldview because you can't help but notice how amazing the world is.

YOU are part of the world – you're amazing too!

Go outside and look down. Find a living, growing, or moving natural thing like an insect, a flower, a blade of grass, or whatever you like.

Don't catch it or pick it – respect its right to be free and alive.

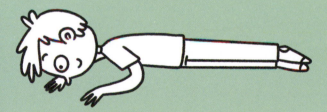

Sit or lie down and focus on watching your natural thing for one or two minutes (or longer if you like). Don't do anything except notice the thing you are looking at.

Look at it as if you are seeing it for the very first time.

Find two more things and repeat the activity.
When you've finished, notice the way you're feeling and describe it here:

SELFIES

Carry out small acts of kindness for people you care about and draw yourself doing them. Write about it if you prefer.

HERE ARE SOME IDEAS:

LET
THEM GO
BEFORE YOU

HOLD A
DOOR OPEN

GIVE A COMPLIMENT

SAY HELLO
TO SOMEONE
NEW

HELP WITH
A CHORE

WRITE THEM A
NOTE OR A CARD

INVITE
SOMEONE NEW
TO PLAY

LET THEM HAVE
THE BEST COOKIE

THINKING POINT:

What do you think your kindness
meant to the other person?

MASTERMIND

Now's your chance to shine.

Write 10 facts you know about something that interests you.

Spend time researching first, or do it straight from memory if you prefer.

THE SUN IS 93 MILLION MILES FROM EARTH

BIRDS CAN'T LIVE IN SPACE

HIPPOS CAN RUN AT 19 MPH

IT RAINS METAL ON VENUS

SPIDERS HAVE EIGHT LEGS

SNAILS CAN SLEEP FOR THREE YEARS

POSITIVE COLORS

Fractals are a natural wonder – just like you.

They occur all over the world and in space.

COLOR THESE
FRACTALS USING
POSITIVE,
BOLD COLORS.

GOAL!

Set yourself a goal – something you'd really like to achieve in the next few weeks.

Maybe you'd like to try something new or push yourself on skills you already have.

WRITE IT HERE

VISUALIZE yourself achieving it – make a mind movie of the moment you get there. Watch it again and this time LISTEN to how loudly your family and friends are celebrating your success.

Watch the mind movie again and FEEL in your body what it will be like to achieve it – from your head to your feet.

BELIEVE you can do this – you've already rewired your brain, so you can be sure it's possible.

BREATHE deeply in and out five times as slowly as you can while you watch it again.

WHAT STEPS DO YOU NEED TO TAKE TO GET READY?

Get out there and **GIVE** it a try!

You've rewired your brain for success – well done! ⟹ You can do this again every time you have a goal. Why not set a goal for next month and next year?

COLOR THIS IN HOWEVER YOU WANT TO:

YES YOU DO

I
DESERVE
LOVE

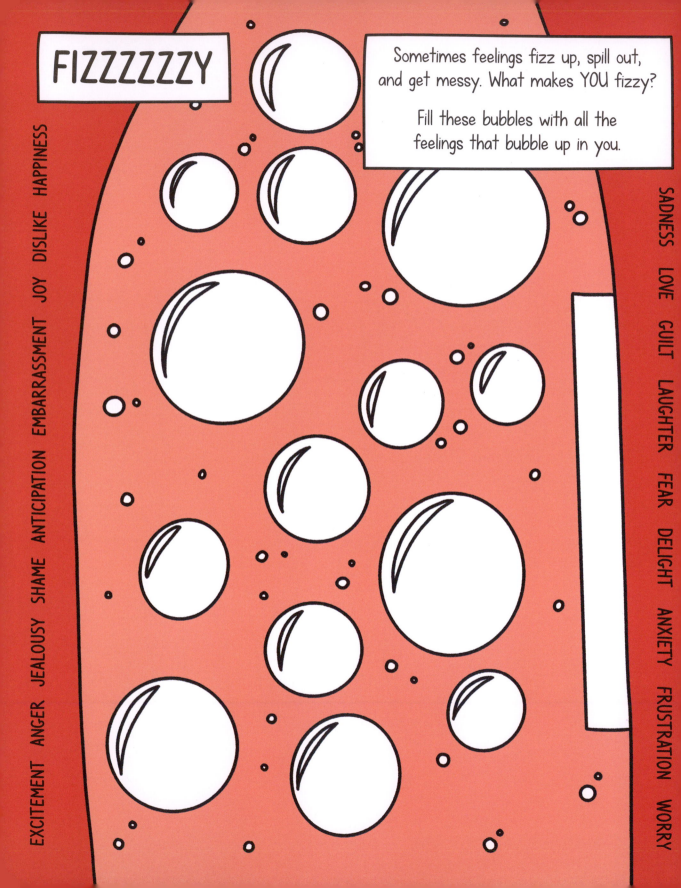

FIZZZZZZY

Sometimes feelings fizz up, spill out, and get messy. What makes YOU fizzy?

Fill these bubbles with all the feelings that bubble up in you.

EXCITEMENT ANGER JEALOUSY SHAME ANTICIPATION EMBARRASSMENT JOY DISLIKE HAPPINESS

SADNESS LOVE GUILT LAUGHTER FEAR DELIGHT ANXIETY FRUSTRATION WORRY

BLAST OFF!

People can say things that put you down or make you doubt yourself. It feels good to get those things blasting off into space and going away forever.

Fill this rocket with the things that get you fired up.

Then count down from 10 to zero.

Now BLAST OFF! and see and hear your rocket disappear out of the atmosphere.

Do you feel confident to challenge yourself to try something new for the first time?

What is it?

_____

_____

_____

Come back and give it a big check when you've done it.

YOU'VE GOT THIS!

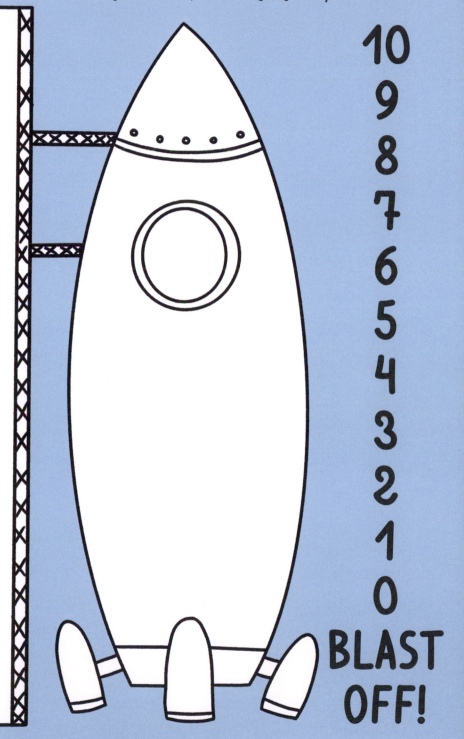

10
9
8
7
6
5
4
3
2
1
0
BLAST OFF!

FEED YOUR SOUL

Try this experiment to really notice what happens when you eat.

You might prefer to do it with a friend or adult.

YOU WILL NEED: • one raisin   and   • one you!

If you don't like raisins, use a blueberry, raspberry, dried cranberry, or a very small piece of chocolate.

MAKE SURE IT'S SOMETHING YOU'RE NOT ALLERGIC TO!

HERE'S WHAT YOU DO:

Sit comfortably and take two or three deep breaths.

Place the raisin in your hand.

Look closely at the raisin with your full attention – imagine that it's like something from another planet that you've never seen before in your life.

Now close your eyes. Place the raisin on one of your fingers and gently move it around on your hand, exploring it carefully.

WHAT DOES THE RAISIN FEEL LIKE?

Hold the raisin near your nose and notice its smell.

Does anything interesting happen in your mouth or tummy?

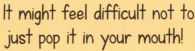 Slowly bring the raisin up to your mouth then rub it across your lips and notice what that feels like.

It might feel difficult not to just pop it in your mouth!

Put the raisin on your tongue and let it sit there for a few seconds. Don't chew it.

Just leave it on your tongue and notice how it feels.

Try not to swallow it just yet.

Wait until the taste fills your mouth, then swallow it.

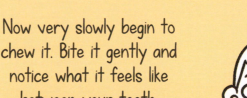 Now very slowly begin to chew it. Bite it gently and notice what it feels like between your teeth.

 Notice your breathing again and then open your eyes.

YOGA

STAR POSE

Try this star pose. It stretches your body in all directions at once.

Doing this pose with a steady and smooth breath will help you feel calm and will improve concentration.

Stretch your legs and feet wide apart, with your toes turned outward. Keep your back, neck, and head straight, and stretch your arms in line with your shoulders with your hands above your feet. Hold and breathe calmly for a minute or two.

TILTED STAR POSE

If you have good balance you can tilt your star – start with the star pose, keeping one leg on the ground, then lower your shoulder on that side while you hold your other foot off the ground.

SPACE ROCKET POSE

This pose will make you feel positive, powerful, and adventurous. Stand up tall and stretch out your spine.

Raise your hands above your head to create the nose of the spaceship.

Lift one foot a little way off the ground and rest it gently on top of the other foot.

Breathe calmly and enjoy the strength in your body. Now change feet and breathe calmly again.

FIVE LITTLE ALIENS

COLOR IN THESE FIVE LITTLE
ALIENS HOWEVER YOU LIKE.

Which of these aliens do you
like the look of most? Why?

_____

_____

Now ask your friends or
family to say which ones
THEY like the look of most.

Does everyone like the
same one or different ones?

_____

_____

_____

THINKING POINT:

What do you notice first
about the way things look?

Check it out the next time
you're out and about,
and write it down here.

BLACK HOLE

Have you ever felt guilty, embarrassed, or ashamed of something?

Maybe it was something someone else said or something you did.

You can learn from these feelings, but you don't need to keep that old moment alive in your mind. You deserve forgiveness, so now's the time to be kind to yourself and then move on.

Write it in this black hole and watch the universe crush it out of existence as you color over it as if it was never there.

You're free! It's gone! Life gets better from here. Notice how relieved and light you feel.

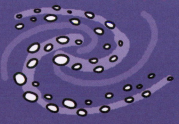

MAKE AMENDS

Give your body some love and care to make up for any mean things you've ever told it.

Put bandages over any part you've said unkind things to, and write something positive about it to make amends and help it feel better.

This activity will rewire your brain to be kinder to yourself.

NOW FIND SOMEONE YOU TRUST TO GIVE YOU A HUG AND HELP YOU FEEL BETTER.

SQUASH THE TOSH

You've got the power to change what you believe about yourself and how you feel.

Push your unhelpful, negative beliefs into this **TOSH SQUASHER** and see what helpful, positive ideas you can pull out of the other side

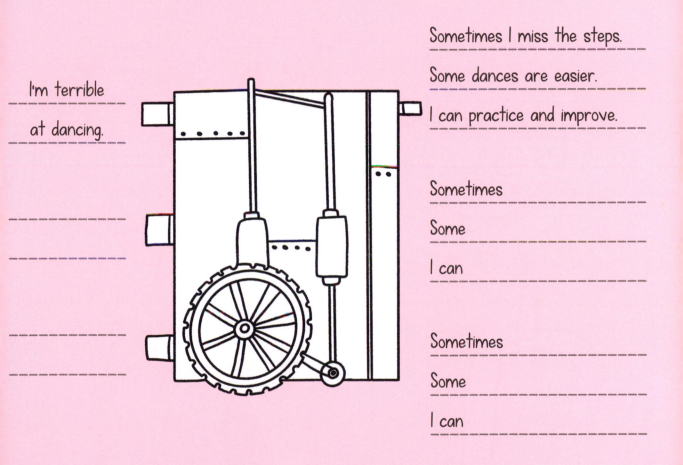

I'm terrible

at dancing.

Sometimes I miss the steps.

Some dances are easier.

I can practice and improve.

Sometimes

Some

I can

Sometimes

Some

I can

Try using your **BE POSITIVE!** power on two of your negative beliefs.

Whenever you feel bad, you know what to do to change how you feel. **SQUASH THE TOSH!**

MOONWALK

Put on your favorite tunes and dance like a visitor from a distant planet.

Teach an Earthling a new dance that you've invented. Make up your own moves, and swing those arms, hands, hips, legs, and feet – in fact, use every bit of you! Do your own thing – THERE ARE NO RULES!

Get your friends and family to join in.

You never know, you could start the next dance craze!

GLITTERY GALAXY

Sometimes everything feels huge.

Focus your attention and bring it all down to a more manageable size with this glittery galaxy jar.

Fill your jar or bottle about halfway with warm water.

Add the glitter glue, then add glitter.

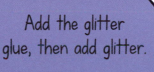

Close the jar or bottle. You can seal the lid with glue for extra protection.

Next, add a few drops of food coloring or a bit of watercolor paint.

SHAKE!!!

Watch as the glitter settles. This will help your feelings to settle too.

Make sure an adult helps you with this activity!

RESPECT YOURSELF

Know yourself to respect yourself.

Fill in these frames with the things that matter to you.

MY HOPES

MY VALUES

Values are what you expect from yourself and others, like kindness, honesty, fairness, trust, loyalty, respect.

Hopes are what you wish for yourself, the people you love, and the world around you.

BE TRUE TO YOURSELF AT ALL TIMES.

Beliefs are the things that you hold true, have faith or confidence in, and are important to you.

MY DREAMS

Dreams are the things you would love to do or be part of.

MY BELIEFS

BOUNDARIES

You deserve respect. If you feel unhappy with how some people treat you, it can affect your self-esteem and your confidence.

You can set boundaries and make decisions about what you're comfortable with in a relationship. If someone is mean to you or leaves you out, you don't have to put up with it. You can ask them to stop and involve a trusted adult if they don't.

I EXPECT PEOPLE
TO BE POLITE

I DESERVE
HONESTY

I DESERVE
KINDNESS

Draw or write how you want to be treated in these planets. Use your own ideas or choose some of the examples. Color in the boundaries around them.

THINKING POINT:

When you feel left out it can hurt as much as a physical injury. Think about a time you felt left out or a time you left someone else out. What did it feel like?

GROW YOUR OWN

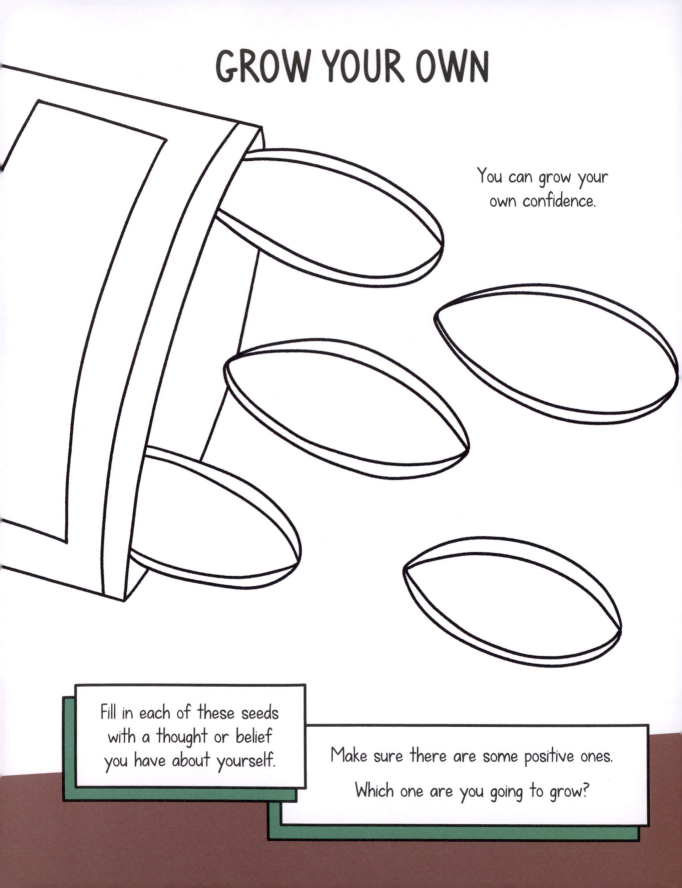

You can grow your own confidence.

Fill in each of these seeds with a thought or belief you have about yourself.

Make sure there are some positive ones.

Which one are you going to grow?

THE ONE YOU FEED IS THE ONE THAT WILL GROW!

Take the seed you'd most like to get rid of, and plant it in this pot without soil, air, water, or light.

Write its name on the label.

Watch it give up and wither away without anything to feed it.

Find two seeds that really need a chance to grow to help you act more confidently. Plant them in these pots and write on the labels.

Cover them in soil, water them, and give them plenty of sunlight.

Color the picture if you like.

Keep coming back to check their progress every time you use this book. As you feel the beliefs growing inside you, draw the stem, leaves, and flowers, and color them in.

When you've grown this strong and healthy belief, what new challenge will you try to test it out?

_____

_____

_____

Come back and give it a big check when you've done the challenge:

MIRROR STICKERS

What do you see when you look in the mirror?

Draw your reflection.

Make sure you ask an adult before you stick them on your mirrors.

What do you feel, think, or believe about your reflection?

What do you feel, think, or believe about yourself?

I see _____

I am _____

My reflection looks _____

After two weeks, come back and describe how different you feel, and what has changed about the way you act.

_____

_____

_____

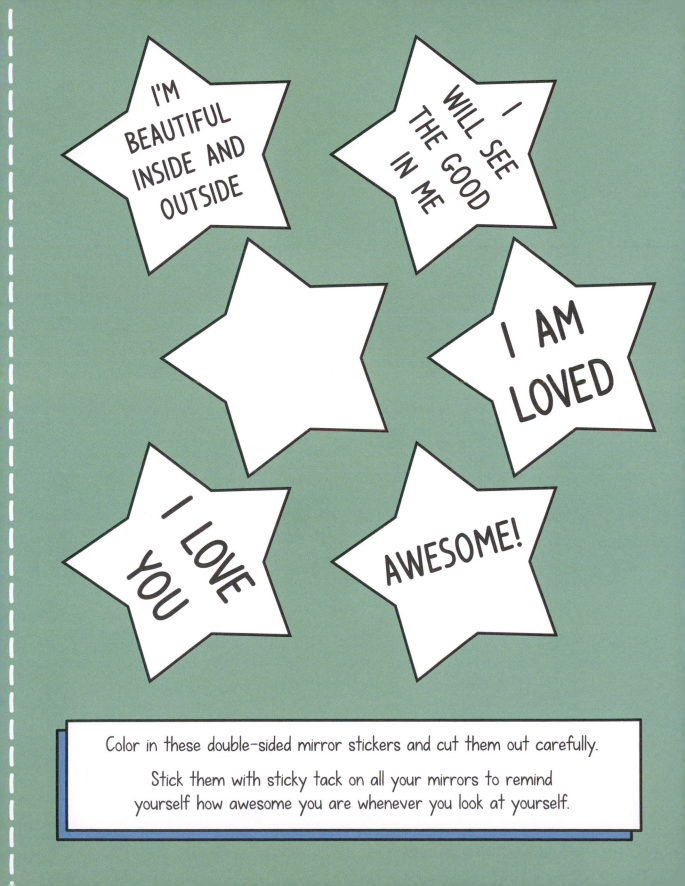

I'M BEAUTIFUL INSIDE AND OUTSIDE

I WILL SEE THE GOOD IN ME

I AM LOVED

I LOVE YOU

AWESOME!

Color in these double-sided mirror stickers and cut them out carefully.

Stick them with sticky tack on all your mirrors to remind yourself how awesome you are whenever you look at yourself.

I AM THE ONE AND ONLY

Everybody's body is unique. Including yours.

Which parts of your body and appearance make you happy?

I like my _____

I love my _____

I respect my _____

I value my _____

My _____ is awesome.

My _____ is wonderful.

THINKING POINT:

What is one thing you wish people knew about you?

STUCK ON YOU

Have you had any sticky moments?

Other people's words and actions can stick to you and keep bothering you.

It's hard to get rid of them.

Stand in this warm rain and enjoy watching them all come unstuck and wash away.

They can dissolve and go into the earth to help beautiful plants and trees to grow.

Write what they were in the raindrops.

You can start fresh now – they aren't stuck on you anymore, so you're free to enjoy your rewired, clear mind.

COLOR THIS IN

NOT

I'M PERFECT

BUT I'M GOOD ENOUGH!

KINDNESS CAPSULE

We all need to feel looked after and loved.

Make yourself a kindness capsule for those days when you're not feeling on top of the world.

Decorate it however you wish with paint, wrapping paper (old comics make excellent wrapping paper!), fabric and ribbons, old posters, magazine pictures – anything that takes your fancy.

YOU WILL NEED:

• A shoebox or something similar (old lunch boxes or ice cream cartons work well)

Fill your capsule with items that will make you happy when you're sad, calm when you're anxious, and busy when you're bored.

Why not make a kindness capsule for a friend, too?

HERE ARE SOME IDEAS:

• soft toys
• modeling clay
• your favorite collector card or toy

• stress ball
• fidget toys
• friendship bracelets

• old ticket
• blowing bubbles
• a small mirror for making faces at yourself

• positive pebbles
• beads
• photos

• puzzle book
• highlighters
• old birthday cards from special people

CLOUD FLYING

Look at this fluffy cloud.

Draw yourself floating on it, feeling completely relaxed, safe, and comfortable.

Imagine, draw, and color the landscape below your cloud.

Your cloud can take you over rivers and lakes, fields and forests, dancing dolphins in sparkling seas, snowy, white mountains, or sizzling deserts. Wherever you want to go.

Spend five minutes imagining yourself calmly and gently flying over your landscape, as if you're really there.

HOW DOES IT FEEL?

If you enjoy this, come back to your cloud whenever you need or want to.

Play some lovely music while you do it if you like.

Fill in these lucky stars and bubbles with the things about yourself that you're thankful for.

I'M THANKFUL
FOR MY SKILL AT

_ _ _ _ _ _ _ _ _

You can also ask your family, friends,
and loved ones for ideas, or ask them to fill in
some stars for you. Add more stars if you want to.

SPACE UNICORNS

We all feel sorry for ourselves and have negative thoughts from time to time.

You might think:

EVERYONE'S PICKING ON YOU	BAD THINGS ONLY HAPPEN TO YOU	PEOPLE WANT TO UPSET YOU	EVERYONE IS MEAN AND UNKIND

You need the space unicorns to help you **BE POSITIVE!**

They've got a few questions for you to answer.

Try them out every time you feel sorry for yourself, and rewire your brain to question your negative thoughts.

You can write down your ideas if it helps.

When things feel really tricky, ask an adult you trust to go through these questions with you.

Then take time for a **TALK 12** together.

Get or give a hug too. You deserve it!

Talk to someone for 12 minutes about anything you like – comics, books, hobbies, sports, fashion, animals, music, and films all make for good conversations.

TALK 12

What's made you feel this way?

Is it true?

What are you basing this on?

Could there be another explanation for what is happening?

Space unicorns can catch your negative thoughts and trap them forever – why not help them?

Ask an adult for some clean, empty jars.

Write your negative thoughts on pieces of paper and trap them inside the jars.

Store them in the dark somewhere, or ask someone to put them out of the way up high in a closet or in a shed.

MISSION POSSIBLE

Some things we can change, and some things we can't. And sometimes we have to learn to live with things we don't like.

It's much easier to do this when you can **BE POSITIVE!** Keep going – you can do it!

List three things you can change, three things you can't change, and three things that will change in time.

A MILLION DREAMS

Fill in these dream bubbles with lovely memories you have of people, places, pets, parties, and picnics.

Or choose absolutely any lovely memory you like. Save some for your future memories if you want. You could add words, drawings, or even photographs.

Why not tell someone about them, describing in as much detail as you can how you felt at the time?

SHOOT FOR THE MOON

We all need to get a good night's sleep.

If you're too tired in the daytime, it's hard to **BE POSITIVE!**

Here are some things you might need for a good night.

A DRINK

FAVORITE TEDDY

A LIGHT SNACK

LISTEN TO A RELAXATION CD

LISTEN TO A BEDTIME STORY

A HUG

Make your own personal list of what YOU need to sleep tight:

NIGHT LIGHT

WARM SOCKS

QUIET

Imagine putting on a space suit when you put on your pajamas so you can quickly go off to sleep and dream about your next mission. If you've got things on your mind, get the space unicorns to pop in and clear your worries away.

As you lie in bed, why not try the breathing exercises from earlier in the book?

HERE'S A REMINDER FOR 3:5 BREATHING

Get comfortable. Notice your body breathing in and out.

After a few breaths, start to count along with yourself, making your in breath last for the count of three and your out breath last for the count of five, breathing smoothly.

Draw yourself tucked up all cozy and sleeping calmly all night long.

HIGH FIVE

Keep your body and brain healthy and happy every day with a high five!

LEARN HOW BY FILLING IN THE MISSING WORDS:

WATER

ENJOY

HEALTH

1. Eat for _____ .

2. Drink _____ .

3. Get plenty of _____ .

4. Get _____ rest and sleep.

EXERCISE

ENOUGH

5. Make sure every day has space to do things you _____ with people who care about you.

TOP TIPS

Our friends need us as much as we need them.

If your friend's self-esteem battery needs charging up with **BE POSITIVE!** power, what advice would you offer?

Make a
**BE POSITIVE!
TOP TIPS**
poster.

THINKING POINT:

Look through this book for ideas and to see which activities you've found the most helpful.

CHECK IN & BLAST OFF

Now that you've learned how to **BE POSITIVE!**
it's time to check in on your battery power.

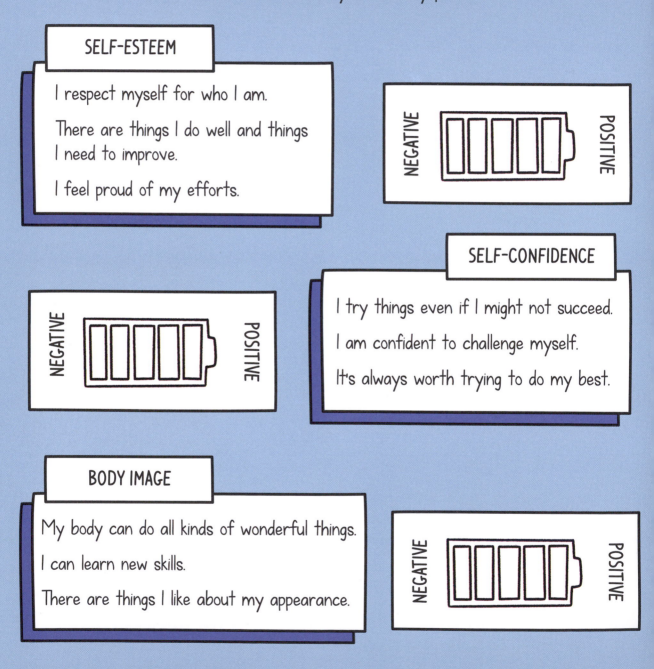

SELF-ESTEEM

I respect myself for who I am.

There are things I do well and things I need to improve.

I feel proud of my efforts.

NEGATIVE | POSITIVE

SELF-CONFIDENCE

I try things even if I might not succeed.

I am confident to challenge myself.

It's always worth trying to do my best.

NEGATIVE | POSITIVE

BODY IMAGE

My body can do all kinds of wonderful things.

I can learn new skills.

There are things I like about my appearance.

NEGATIVE | POSITIVE

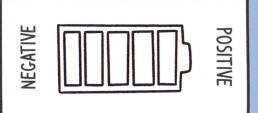

NEGATIVE | POSITIVE

Good things do happen.

Some people are really kind.

I can have fun and go to interesting places.

Compare the power in your batteries now with the ones at the start of the book.

What has improved?

What do you need to keep working at?

Don't forget you can go back and do any of these activities again, as often as you like.

THINKING POINT:

Challenge yourself to try one new thing now that you can BE POSITIVE!

Write it down with any steps you need to think about to get there:

YOU'RE AMAZING!
TRUST YOURSELF

IT'S TIME TO BLAST OFF! GO YOU!

THE PAGE FOR GROWN-UPS

This activity book is perfect for parents, caregivers, teachers, learning mentors, therapists, social workers, and youth leaders who want to help children to believe in themselves and others and develop positive body image, self-esteem, and confidence.

Modern life bombards children with ideals of success, popularity, and perfection alongside the everyday message to be better and do better as they grow, make mistakes, and learn. Internal and external pressures can cause them to compare themselves with others and feel they aren't good enough, which damages confidence in themselves, their developing bodies, and the world around them. Children may become overwhelmed and struggle to make sense of what is happening without the language or tools to explain their distress. You might notice an increase in self-doubt and negative thoughts, along with complaints of stomachaches, headaches, or tiredness, and avoidance of previously enjoyed activities.

In a loving and nurturing environment, children are resilient and will often work through problems without needing additional help. This book enables your child to explore, express, and explain their self-doubts and open up the conversation with you. The fun activities increase positivity, confidence, self-esteem, and self-belief, build further resilience, combat negative thoughts and expectations, and encourage a heathy sense of themselves and their world.

If your child's lack of confidence persists beyond three months or escalates rather than decreases, talk to their school, your doctor, a counselor, or one of the organizations listed below for support and guidance.

NATIONAL ALLIANCE ON MENTAL ILLNESS (NAMI)

Educate, advocate, listen, lead.

The NAMI HelpLine can be reached Monday through Friday, 10 am-6 pm, ET.

NAMI is the nation's largest grassroots mental health organization dedicated to building better lives for the millions of Americans affected by mental illness.

www.nami.org

Tel: 1-800-950-NAMI (6264)

info@nami.org

GOODTHERAPY.ORG®

Helping people find therapists. Advocating for ethical therapy.

GoodTherapy.org offers a directory to help you in your search for a therapist. Using the directory, you can search by therapist location, specialization, gender, and age group treated. If you search by location, your results will include the therapists near you and will display their credentials, location, and the issues they treat.

Tel: 1-888-563-2112 ext. 1

www.goodtherapy.org

NATIONAL PARENT HELPLINE

Support and resources for parents worried about their children.

Tel: 1-855-4A PARENT (1-855-427-2736)

www.nationalparenthelpline.org

DR. SHARIE COOMBES